Charles Summer

The One Man Power vs. Congress!

Charles Summer

The One Man Power vs. Congress!

ISBN/EAN: 9783337036843

Printed in Europe, USA, Canada, Australia, Japan

Cover: Foto ©Suzi / pixelio.de

More available books at **www.hansebooks.com**

THE ONE MAN POWER vs. CONGRESS!

ADDRESS

OF

HON. CHARLES SUMNER,

AT THE

MUSIC HALL, BOSTON,

OCTOBER 2, 1866.

BOSTON:

WRIGHT & POTTER, STATE PRINTERS,

No. 4 SPRING LANE.

1866.

ADDRESS.

Mr. President:—

It is now more than a year since I last had the honor of addressing my fellow-citizens of Massachusetts. On that occasion I dwelt on what seemed to be the proper policy towards the States recently in rebellion—insisting that it was our duty, while renouncing indemnity for the past, to obtain at least security for the future ; and this security, I maintained, could be found only in the exclusion of ex-rebels from political power, and in irreversible guarantees especially applicable to the national creditor and the national freedman. During the intervening months, the country has been agitated by this question, which was perplexed by an unexpected difference between the President and Congress. The President insists upon installing ex-rebels in political power, and sets at naught the claim of guarantees and the idea of security for the future, while he denies to Congress any control over this question, and takes it all to himself. Congress has asserted its control, and has endeavored to shut out ex-rebels from political power and to establish guarantees, to the end that there might be security for the future. Meanwhile, the States recently in rebellion, with the exception of Tennessee, are without representation in Congress. Thus stands the case.

The Two Parties in the Controversy.

The two parties in the controversy are the President on the one side, and the people of the United States in Congress assembled on the other side : the first representing the Executive ; the second representing the Legislative. It is the *One Man Power* vs. *Congress.* Of course, each of these performs its part in the government ; but, until now, it has always been supposed that the Legislative *gave the law* to the Executive, and not that the Executive *gave the law* to the Legislative. Perhaps this irrational assumption becomes more astonishing when it is considered that the actual President, besides being the creature of an accident, is inferior in ability and character, while the House of Representatives is eminent in both respects. A President, who has already sunk below any other president, even Buchanan, madly undertakes to give the law to a House of Representatives, which, there is reason to believe, is the best that has sat since the formation of the Constitution. Thus, in looking at the parties, we are tempted to exclaim : Such a Presid͏͏ dictating to such a Congress ! It was said of Gustavus Adolphus that he had drilled the Diet of Sweden to vote or be silent at the word of command; but Andrew Johnson is not Gustavus Adolphus, and the American Congress is not the Diet of Sweden.

Irreversible Guarantees must be had.

The question at issue is one of the vastest ever presented for practical decision, involving the name and weal of this Republic at home and abroad. It is not a military question; it is a question of statesmanship. We are to secure by counsel what was won by war. Failure now will make the war itself a failure; surrender now will undo all our victories. Let the President prevail, and straightway the plighted faith of the Republic will be broken; the national creditor and the national freedman will be sacrificed; the Rebellion itself will flaunt its insulting power; the whole country, in length and breadth, will be disturbed; and the rebel region will be handed over to misrule and anarchy. Let Congress prevail and all this will be reversed; the plighted faith of the Republic will be preserved; the national creditor and the national freedman will be protected; the Rebellion itself will be trampled out forever; the whole country, in length and breadth, will be at peace; and the rebel region, no longer harassed by controversy and degraded by injustice, will enjoy the richest fruits of security and reconciliation. To labor for this cause may well tempt the young and rejoice the old.

And now, to-day, I protest again against any admission of ex-rebels to the great partnership of this Republic, and I renew the claim of irreversible guarantees especially applicable to the national creditor and the national freedman; insisting now, as I did a year ago, that it is our duty, while renouncing indemnity for the past, to obtain at least security for the future. At the close of a terrible war—which has wasted our treasure—which has murdered our fellow-citizens—which has filled the land with funerals—which has maimed and wounded multitudes whom death had spared—and which has broken up the very foundations of peace—our first duty is to provide safeguards for the future. This can be only by provisions, sure, fundamental and irrepealable, which shall fix forever the results of the war—the obligations of government—and the equal rights of all. Such is the suggestion of common prudence and of self-defence, as well as of common honesty. To this end we must make haste slowly. States which precipitated themselves out of Congress must not be permitted to precipitate themselves back. They must not be allowed to enter those halls which they treasonably deserted, until we have every reasonable assurance of future good conduct. We must not admit them, and then repent our folly. Those words, once used in the British Parliament and revived by Mr. Webster, furnish the key to our duty:—

> "I hear a lion in the lobby roar;
> Say, Mr. Speaker, shall I shut the door ?
> Or shall we rather let the monster in,
> Then see if we can shut him out again ?"

I am against letting the monster in, until he is no longer terrible in mouth or paw.

No Unnecessary Delay.

But while holding this ground, I desire to disclaim every sentiment of vengeance or punishment, and also every thought of delay or procrastination. Here I do not yield to the President or to any other person. Nobody can be more anxious than I am to see this chasm closed forever.

There is a long way and a short way. There is a long time and a short time. If there be any whose policy is for the longest way or for the longest time, I am not of the number. I am for the shortest way and also for the shortest time. And I object to the interference of the President, because, whether intentionally or unintentionally, he interposes delay and keeps the chasm open. More than all others, the President, by his officious assumptions, has lengthened the way and lengthened the time. Of this there can be no doubt.

A Lost Opportunity.

From all quarters we learn that after the surrender of Lee, the rebels were ready for any terms, if they could escape with their lives. They were vanquished, and they knew it. The rebellion was crushed, and they knew it. They hardly expected to save a small fraction of their property. They did not expect to save their political power. They were too sensible not to see that participants in rebellion could not pass at once into the partnership of government. They made up their minds to exclusion. They were submissive. There was nothing they would not do, *even to the extent of enfranchising their freedmen and providing for them homesteads*. Had the national government merely taken advantage of this plastic condition, it might have stamped Equal Rights upon the whole people, as upon molten wax, while it fixed the immutable conditions of permanent peace. The question of reconstruction would have been settled before it arose. It is sad to think that this was not done. Perhaps in all history there is no instance of such an opportunity lost. Truly should our country say in penitential supplication ; " We have left undone those things which we ought to have done ; and we have done those things which we ought not to have done."

Do not take this on my authority. Listen to those on the spot, who have seen with their own eyes. A brave officer of our army wrote to me from Alabama, as follows : —

" I believe the mass of the people could have been easily controlled, if none of the excepted classes had received pardon. These classes did not expect anything more than life, and even feared for that. Let me condense the whole subject. At the surrender, the South could have been moulded at will; but it is now as stiff-necked and rebellious as ever."

In the same vein another officer testifies from Texas, as follows :

"There is one thing, however, that is making against the speedy return of quietness, not only in this State, but throughout the entire South, and *that is the reconstruction policy of President Johnson.* It is doing more to unsettle this country than people who are not practical observers of its workings have any idea of. Before this policy was made known the people were prepared to accept any thing. They expected to be treated as rebels, their leaders being punished and the property of others confiscated. But the moment it was made known all their assurance returned. Rebels have again become arrogant and exacting; treason stalks through the land unabashed."

This testimony might be multiplied indefinitely. From city and country, from highway and byway there is but one voice. When, therefore, the President, in opprobrious terms, complains of Congress as interposing delay, I reply to him, " No, Sir, it is you, who by unexpected and most perverse assumptions, have put off the glad day of security and reconciliation, which is so much longed for. It is you, who have inaugurated anew that *malignant sectionalism*, which, so long as it exists, will keep this Union divided in fact, if not in name. Sir, you are the Disunionist."

The Presidential Policy founded on two Blunders.

Glance, if you please, at that Presidential Policy—so constantly called " my policy "—which is now so vehemently pressed upon the country, and you will find that it pivots on at least two alarming blunders, as can be easily seen; *first*, in setting up the *One Man Power*, as the source of jurisdiction over this great question; and *secondly*, in using the *One Man Power* for the restoration of rebels to place and influence, so that good Unionists, whether white or black, are rejected, and the rebellion itself is revived in the new governments. Each of these assumptions is an enormous blunder. You will see that I use a mild term to characterize such a double-headed usurpation.

The One Man Power.

(1.) Pray, Sir, where in the Constitution do you find any sanction of the *One Man Power* as the source of this extraordinary jurisdiction ? I had always supposed that the President was the Executive, bound to see the laws faithfully executed ; but not empowered to make laws. The Constitution expressly says : " The Executive Power shall be vested in a President of the United States of America." But the Legislative Power is elsewhere. According to the Constitution ; " All Legislative Powers herein granted shall be vested in a Congress of the United States, which shall consist of a Senate and House of Representatives." And yet the President has assumed legislative power, even to the extent of making laws and constitutions for States. You all know that at the close of the war, when the rebel States were without lawful governments, he assumed to supply them. In this business of reconstruction he assumed to determine who should vote, and also to affix conditions for adoption by the conventions. Look, if you please, at the character of this assumption. The President, from the executive mansion at Washington, reaches his long executive arm into certain States and dictates their constitutions. Surely there is nothing executive in this assumption. It is not even military. It is legislative, pure and simple, and nothing else. It is an attempt by the *One Man Power* to do what can be done only by the legislative branch of the government. And yet so perverse is the President in absorbing to himself all power over the reconstruction of the rebel States, that he insists that Congress must accept his work without addition or subtraction. He can impose conditions; Congress cannot. He can determine who shall vote; Congress cannot. His jurisdiction is not only complete, but exclusive. If all this be so, then has our President a most extraordinary power, never before dreamed of. He may exclaim with Louis XIV.: "The State, it is I;" while, like this magnificent king, he sacrifices the innocent, and repeats that fatal crime, the revocation of the edict of Nantes. His whole "policy" is a "revocation" of all that has been promised, and all that we have a right to expect.

Here it is well to note a distinction, which is not without importance in the discussion of the issue between the President and Congress. Nobody doubts that the President may during war govern any conquered territory as commander-in-chief, and for this purpose he may detail any military officer as military governor. But it is one thing to govern a State temporarily by military power, and quite another thing to create a constitution for a State which shall continue *when the military power has expired.* The former is a military act, and belongs to the President. The latter is a civil act, and belongs to Congress. On this distinction I stand, and this is not the first time that I have asserted it. Of course, the governments set up in this illegitimate way are necessarily illegitimate, except so far as they may acquire validity from time or subsequent recognition. It needs no learned chief justice of North Carolina solemnly to declare this. It is manifest from the nature of the case.

But this illegitimacy becomes still more manifest, when it is known that the constitutions which the President orders and tries to cram upon Congress have never been submitted to a popular vote. Each is the naked offspring of an illegitimate convention called into being by the President, in the exercise of an illegitimate power.

There is another provision of the Constitution, by which, according to a judgment of the Supreme Court of the United

States, this question is referred to Congress and not to the President. I refer to the provision that " *the United States* shall guarantee to every State in this Union, a republican government." On these words Chief Justice Taney, speaking for the Supreme Court, has adjudged, "that it rests with Congress to decide what government is the established one in a State ; as *the United States* guarantee to each State a republican government, *Congress must necessarily decide what government is established in a State* before it can determine whether it is republican or not; and that undoubtedly a military government established as the permanent government of a State would not be a republican government, and it would be the duty of Congress to overthrow it." (Luther *vs.* Borden, 7 Howard, Rep. 42.) But the President sets at naught this commanding text of the Constitution, reinforced by this positive judgment of the Supreme Court, and claims this extraordinary power for himself, to the exclusion of Congress. He is " the United States." In him the Republic is manifest. He can do all. Congress can do nothing.

And now the whole country is summoned by the President to recognize State governments created by constitutions thus illegitimate in origin and character. Without considering if they contain the proper elements of security for the future, or if they are republican in form ; and without any inquiry into the validity of their adoption ;—nay, in the very face of testimony, showing that they contain no elements of security for the future—that they are not republican in form—and that they have never been adopted by the loyal people, we are commanded to accept them ; and when we hesitate, the President himself, leading the outcry, assails us with angry vituperation, blunted, it must be confessed, by a coarseness without precedent and without bounds. It is well that such a cause has such an advocate.

In thus setting up the *One Man Power* as a source of jurisdiction over this great question, the President has committed a blunder of constitutional law, proceeding from an immense egotism, in which the little pronoun " I " plays a gigantic part. It is " I," *vs.* the people of the United States in Congress assembled. On this unnatural blunder I might say more ; but I have said enough. My present purpose is accomplished if I make you see it clearly.

Giving Power to Ex-Rebels.

(2.) The other blunder is of a different character. It is giving power to ex-rebels, at the expense of constant Unionists, white or black, and employing them in the work of reconstruction, so that the new governments continue to represent the rebellion. This same blunder, when committed by one of the heroes of the war, was promptly overruled by the President himself; but Andrew Johnson now does what Sherman was not allowed to do. The blunder is strange and unaccountable.

Here the evidence is constant and cumulative. It begins with his first proclamation, which was for the reconstruction of North Carolina. Holden was appointed Provisional Governor, an office unknown to the law, and for which there was no provision, although it was notorious that he had been a member of the convention which adopted the Act of secession, and that he himself had signed it. Then came Perry, Provisional Governor of South Carolina, who, besides holding a judicial station under the rebel government, was one of its Commissioners of Impressments. I have a rebel newspaper containing one of his advertisements in the latter character. There also was Parsons, Provisional Governor of Alabama, who in 1863 introduced into the legislature of that State formal resolutions tendering to Jefferson Davis "hearty thanks for his good labors in the cause of our common country, together with the assurance of continued support;" and afterwards, in 1864, denounced our national debt, exclaiming in the legislature, " Does any sane man suppose we will consent to pay their [the United States,] war debt, contracted in sending armies and navies to burn our towns and cities, to lay waste our country, whose soldiers have robbed and murdered our peaceful inhabitants?" Such were the men appointed by the President to institute loyal governments. But this selection becomes more strange and unaccountable when it is considered that all this was done in defiance of law.

There is a recent enactment of Congress, which requires that no person shall be appointed to any office of the United States, unless such office has been created by law. And there is another enactment of Congress, which provides that all officers, civil or military, before entering upon their official duties or receiving any salary or compensation, shall take an oath declaring that they have held no office under the Rebellion or given any aid thereto. In the face of these enactments, which are sufficiently explicit, the President began his work of reconstruction by appointing civilians to an office absolutely unknown to the law, when besides they could not take the required oath of office ; and to complete the disregard of Congress he fixed their salary and paid it out of the funds of the War Department.

Of course such a proceeding was an instant encouragement and license to all ex-rebels, no matter how much blood was on their hands. Rebellion was at a premium. It was easy to see, that if these men were good enough to be governors of States, in defiance of Congress, all others in the same political predicament would be good enough for the inferior offices. And it was so. From top to bottom these States were organized by men who had been warring on their country. Ex-rebels were appointed by the governors or chosen by the people everywhere. Ex-rebels sat in conventions and in legislatures. Ex-rebels became judges, justices of the peace, sheriffs and everything else, while the faithful Unionist, white or black, was rejected. As with Cordelia, his

2

love was " according to his bond, nor more nor less;" but all this was of no avail. How often during the war have I pleaded for such patriots and urged you to every effort for their redemption ; and now, when our arms have prevailed, it is they who are cast down while the enemies of the Republic are exalted. The pirate Semmes returns from his ocean cruise to be chosen Probate Judge in Alabama. In New Orleans the rebel mayor at the time the city surrendered to the national flag is once more mayor, and employs his regained power in that terrible massacre which rises in judgment against the presidential policy. Persons are returned to Congress, whose service in the rebellion makes it impossible for them to take the oath of office, as in the case of Georgia, which selects as senators Herschell V. Johnson, who was a senator of the rebel Congress, and Alexander H. Stephens, the vice-president of the rebellion. These are but instances; but from these you may learn all.

There is nothing in the reach of the President which he has not lavished on ex-rebels. The power of pardon and amnesty, like the power of appointment, has been used for them, by wholesale and retail. It would have been easy to affix a condition to every pardon, requiring that, before it took effect, the recipient should carve out of his estate a homestead for every one of his freedmen, and thus secure to each what they all covet so much, a piece of land. But the President did no such thing, although, in the words of the old writ, " often requested so to do." Such a condition would have helped the loyal freedman, rather than the rebel master. In the same spirit, while undertaking to determine who shall be voters, all colored persons, howsoever loyal, were disfranchised, while all white persons, except certain specified classes, although black with rebellion, were constituted voters on taking a simple oath of allegiance, thus giving to ex-rebels a prevailing power.

Partisans of the Presidential " policy " are in the habit of declaring that it is a continuation of the policy of the martyred Lincoln. This is a mistake. Would that he could rise from his bloody shroud to repel the calumny ! But he has happily left his testimony behind, in words which all who have ears to hear can hear. On one occasion the martyr presented the truth bodily when he said, in a suggestive metaphor, that we must " build up from the sound materials ;" but his successor insists upon building from materials rotten with treason and gaping with rebellion. On another occasion the martyr said that " an attempt to guarantee and protect a *revived* State government, constructed in whole or in *preponderating part* from the *very element* against whose hostility and violence it is to be protected, is *simply absurd.*" But this is the very thing which the President is now attempting. He is constructing State governments, not merely in preponderating part, *but in whole* from the hostile element. Therefore, he departs openly from the policy of the martyred Lincoln.

The martyr says to his successor that his policy is " simply absurd." He is right, although he might say more than this. Its absurdity is too apparent. It is as if, in abolishing the Inquisition, the inquisitors had been continued under another name, and Torquemada had received a fresh license for cruelty. It is as if King William, after the overthrow of James II., had made the infamous Jeffries Lord Chancellor. Common sense and common justice cry out against the outrage ; and yet this is the Presidential " policy " now so passionately commended to the American people.

Government, according to Aristotle, is a " partnership," and I accept this term as especially applicable to our government. And now the President, in the exercise of the *One Man Power*, decrees that communities lately in rebellion shall be taken at once into our " partnership." I object to the decree as dangerous to the Republic. I am not against pardon, clemency or magnanimity, except where they are at the expense of good men. I trust that they will always be practised ; but I insist that recent rebels shall not be admitted without proper precautions to the business of the firm. And I insist also that the *One Man Power* shall not be employed to force them into the firm.

The President inconsistent with Himself.

Such are two pivotal blunders of the President. It is not easy to see how he has fallen into these—so strong were his early professions the other way. The powers of Congress he had distinctly admitted. Thus, as early as 24th July, 1865, he had sent to Sharkey, acting by his appointment as Provisional Governor of Mississippi, this despatch : " It must, however, be distinctly understood, that the restoration to which your proclamation refers *will be subject to the will of Congress*." Nothing could be more positive ; and he was equally positive against the restoration of rebels to power. You do not forget that, in accepting his nomination as Vice-President, he rushed forward to declare that the rebel States must be remodelled ; that confiscation must be enforced, and that rebels must be excluded from the work of reconstruction. His language was plain and unmistakable. Announcing that " government must be fixed on the principles of *eternal justice*," he went on to declare, that, " if the man who gave his influence and his means to destroy the government should be permitted to participate in the great work of reorganization, then all the precious blood so freely poured out will have been wantonly spilled, and all our victories go for naught." True ; very true. Then, in words of surpassing energy, he cried out, that " the great plantations must be seized and divided into small farms," and that " traitors should take a back seat in the work of restoration." Perhaps the true rule was never expressed with more homely and vital force than in this last saying, often repeated in different forms : " For rebels, back seats." Add to this that other saying so often repeated, " treason must be made odious," and you have two great principles of a just reconstruction, once proclaimed by the President, but now practically disowned by him.

How the President fell.

You will ask how the President fell. This is hard to say, certainly, without much plainness of speech. Mr. Seward openly confesses that he counselled the present fatal " policy." Unquestionably Mr. Blair, father and son, did the same. So also, I doubt not, did Mr. Preston King. It is easy to see that Mr. Seward was not a wise counsellor. This is not his first costly blunder. In formal despatches he early announced that " the rights of the States and the condition of every human being will remain subject to exactly the same laws and forms of administration, whether the revolution shall succeed or whether it shall fail." And now he labors for the fulfilment of his own prophecy. Obviously from the beginning he has failed to comprehend the rebellion, while in his nature he is abnormal and eccentric, jumping like the knight on the chess board, rather than moving on straight lines. Undoubtedly the influence of such a man over the President has not been good. But the President himself has been his own worst counsellor, as he has been his own worst defender. He does not open his mouth without furnishing evidence against himself.

The brave words with which he accepted his nomination as Vice-President resounded through the country. He was elected. Then followed two scenes, each of which filled the people with despair. The first was of the new Vice-President taking the oath of office—in the presence of the foreign ministers, the judges of the Supreme Court, and the Senate—while in such a condition that his attempted speech became trivial and incoherent, and he did not know the name of the Secretary of the Navy, who is now the devoted supporter of his policy, as he has been his recent travelling companion. One month and one week afterwards President Lincoln was assassinated. The people, wrapt in affliction at the great tragedy, trembled as they beheld a drunken man ascend the heights of power. But they were generous and forgiving—almost forgetful. He was our President, and hands were outstretched to welcome and sustain him. His early utterances as President although common-place, loose and wordy, gave assurance that the rebellion and its authors would find little favor from him. Treason was to be made odious.

Personal Relations with the President.

It was at this time that my own relations with him commenced. I had known him slightly while he was in the [Senate ; but I lost no time in seeing him after he became President. He received me kindly. I hope that I shall not err, if I allude briefly to what passed between us. You are my constituents and I wish you to know the mood of the President at that time and also what your representative attempted.

I was in Washington during the first month of the new administration, destined to fill such an unhappy place in history. During this period I saw the President frequently, sometimes at the private house he then occupied, and sometimes at his office in the treasury. On these occasions the constant topic was "reconstruction," which was considered in every variety of aspect. More than once I ventured to press upon him the duty and the renown of carrying out the principles of the Declaration of Independence and of founding the new governments in the rebel States on the consent of the governed, without any distinction of color. To this earnest appeal he replied on one occasion, as I sat with him alone, in words which I can never forget: "On this question, Mr. Sumner, there is no difference between us. You and I are alike." Need I say, that I was touched to the heart by this annunciation, which seemed to promise a victory without a battle. Accustomed to controversy, I saw clearly that if the President declared himself in favor of the Equal Rights of All, the good cause must prevail without controversy. After expressing to him my joy and gratitude, I remarked still further, that it was important that there should be no division in the great Union party—that there should be no line run through it, on one side of which would be gentlemen calling themselves "the President's friends," but that we should be kept all together as one seamless garment. To this he promptly replied: "I mean to keep you all together." Nothing could be better. We were to be kept all together on the principle of Equal Rights. As I walked away from the President that evening, the battle of my life seemed to be ended, while the Republic rose before me, refulgent in the blaze of assured Freedom, an example to the nations.

On another occasion, during the same period, the case of Tennessee was discussed. I expressed the hope most earnestly that the President would use his influence directly for the establishment of impartial suffrage in that State, saying that in this way Tennessee would be put at the head of the returning column and be made an example; in one word, that all the other States would be obliged to dress on Tennessee. The President replied, that if he were at Nashville, he would see that this was accomplished. I could not help rejoining promptly, that he need not be at Nashville, for at Washington his hand was on the long end of the lever with which he could easily move all Tennessee; referring of course to the powerful but legitimate influence which the President might exercise in his own State by the expression of his desires. Let me confess that his hesitation on this occasion disturbed me; but I attributed it to an unnecessary caution rather than to any infidelity. He had been so positive with me, how could I suspect him!

On other occasions the conversation was renewed. Such was my interest in this question, that I could not see the President without introducing it. As I was about to return home, I said that I desired, even at the risk of repetition, to make some parting suggestions on the constant topic, and that, with his permission, I would proceed point by point, as was the habit of the pulpit in former days. He smiled and said pleasantly, "Have I not always listened to you?" I replied, "You have, and I am grateful." After remarking that the rebel region was still in military occupation and that it was the plain duty of the President to use his temporary power for the establishment of correct principles, I proceeded to say : First ; See to it that no newspaper is allowed which is not thoroughly loyal and does not speak well of the National Government and of Equal Rights; and here I reminded him of the saying of the Duke of Wellington, that in a place under martial law, an unlicensed press was as impossible as on the deck of a ship of war. Secondly ; Let the officers that you send, as military governors or otherwise, be known for their devotion to Equal Rights, so that their names alone will be a proclamation, while their simple presence will help educate the people ; and here I mentioned Major-General Carl Schurz, who still held his commission in the army, as such a person. Thirdly ; Encourage the population to resume the profitable labors of agriculture, commerce and manufactures without delay ; but for the present to avoid politics. Fourthly ; Keep the whole rebel region under these good influences, and, at the proper moment, hand over the subject of reconstruction with the great question of Equal Rights, to the judgment of Congress, where it belongs. All this the President received at the time with perfect kindness, and I mention this with the more readiness because I remember to have seen in the papers a very different statement.

Only a short time afterwards there was a change, which seemed like a summerset or an apostacy ; and then ensued a strange sight. Instead of faithful Unionists, recent rebels thronged the Presidential ante-chambers, rejoicing in a new-found favor. They made speeches at the President, and he made speeches at them. A mutual sympathy was manifest. On one occasion the President announced himself a "Southern man," with "Southern sympathies," thus quickening that *sectional* flame which good men hoped to see quenched forever. Alas ! if after all our terrible sacrifices we are still to have a President who does not know how to spurn every sectional appeal and make himself the representative of all ! Unhappily, whatever the President said or did was *sectional*. He showed himself constantly a *sectionalist*. Instead of telling the ex-rebels that thronged the Presidential ante-chambers, as he should have done, that he was their friend ; that he wished them well from the bottom of his heart ; that he longed to see their fields yield an increase and peace in all their borders, and that, to this end, he counselled them to devote themselves to agriculture, commerce and manufactures, and for the present to say nothing about politics;—instead of this, he sent them away talking and thinking of nothing but politics, and frantic for the re-establishment of a sectional power. Instead of designating officers of the army as military governors, which I had supposed he would do, he appointed ex-rebels, who could not take the oath required by Congress of all officers of the United States, and they in turn appointed ex-rebels to office under them, so that participation in the rebellion found its reward, and treason, instead of being made odious, became a passport to power. Everywhere ex-rebels came out of their hiding-places. They walked the streets defiantly, and asserted their old domination. Under the auspices of the President, a new campaign was planned against the Republic, and they who failed in open war now sought to enter the very citadel of political power. Victory, purchased by so much loyal blood and treasure, was little better than a cipher. Slavery itself revived in the spirit of Caste. Faithful men who had been trampled down by the Rebellion were trampled down still more by these Presidential governments. For the Unionist there was no liberty of the press or liberty of speech, and the lawlessness of slavery began to rage anew.

Every day brought tidings that the rebellion was re-appearing in its essential essence. Amidst all professions of submission there was an immitigable hate to the National Government, and a prevailing injustice to the freedman. This was last autumn. I was then in Boston. Moved by a desire to arrest this fatal tendency, I appealed by letter to members of the Cabinet, entreating. them to stand firm against a " policy " which promised nothing but disaster. As soon as the elections were over I appealed directly to the President himself, by a telegraphic despatch, as follows:—

BOSTON, 12th Nov., 1865.

To the President of the United States, Washington:

As a faithful friend and supporter of your administration, I most respectfully petition you to suspend for the present your policy towards the rebel States. I should not present this prayer if I were not painfully convinced that thus far it has failed to obtain any reasonable guarantees for that security in the future which is essential to peace and reconciliation. To my mind, it abandons the freedmen to the control of their ancient masters; and leaves the national debt exposed to repudiation by returning rebels. The Declaration of Independence asserts the Equality of all men, and that rightful government can be founded only on the consent of the governed. I see small chance of peace unless these great principles are practically established. Without this the house will continue divided against itself. CHARLES SUMNER,
Senator of the United States.

On reaching Washington Saturday evening, immediately before the opening of the last session of Congress, I lost no time in seeing the President. I was with him that evening three hours. I found him changed in temper and purpose. How unlike that President, who, only a few days after his arrival at power, had made me feel so happy in the assurances of agreement on the great question before the country! He was no longer sympathetic or even kindly, but harsh, petulant and unreasonable. Plainly, his heart was with the ex-rebels. For the Unionist, white or black, who had borne the burthen of the day, he had little feeling. Perversely he would not see the bad spirit of the rebel States, and he insisted that the outrages there were insufficient to justify their exclusion from Congress. It was in this connection, that the following dialogue ensued : *The President.*—" Are there no murders in Massachusetts?" *Mr. S.*—" Unhappily, yes ; sometimes." *The President.*—" Are there no assaults in Boston? Do not men there, sometimes, knock each other down, so that the police is obliged to interfere?" *Mr. S.*—" Unhappily, yes." *The President.*—" Would you consent that Massachusetts, on this account, should be excluded from Congress?" *Mr. S.*—" No, Mr. President, I would not." And here I stopped, without remarking on the entire irrelevancy of the inquiry. I left the President that night with the painful conviction that his whole soul was set as flint against the good cause, and that by the assassination of Abraham Lincoln the Rebellion had vaulted into the Presidential chair. Jefferson Davis was then in the casemates at Fortress Monroe, but Andrew Johnson was doing his work.

> " Ah ! what avails it, ——
> If the gulled conqueror receives the chain,
> And flattery subdues when arms are vain."

From this time forward I was not in doubt as to his " policy," which asserted a condition of things in the rebel region inconsistent with the terrible truth. It was, therefore, natural that I should characterize one of his messages, covering over the enormities there, as " whitewashing.". This mild term was thought by some at the time to be too strong. Subsequent events have shown that it was too weak. The whole rebel region is little better than a " whited sepulchre." It is that saddest of all sepulchres, the sepulchre of Human Rights. The dead men's bones are the remains of faithful Union soldiers, dead on innumerable fields or stifled in the pens of Andersonville and Belle-isle ; also of constant Unionists, white and black, whom we are sacredly bound to protect, now murdered on highways and byways, or slaughtered at Memphis and New Orleans. The uncleanness is injustice, wrong and outrage of the most loathsome character. And the President is engaged in " whiting" over these things, so that they shall not be seen by the American people. To do this he has garbled a despatch of Sheridan and has abused the hospitality of the country by a travelling speech, where every word that was not foolish, vulgar and vindictive, was a vain attempt at " whitewashing."

The Presidential Madness.

Meanwhile the Presidential madness has become more than ever manifest. It has shown itself in frantic efforts to defeat the Constitutional Amendment proposed by Congress for adoption by the people. By this amendment certain safeguards are established. Citizenship is defined, and protection is assured at least in what are called civil rights. The basis of representation is fixed on the number of voters, so that if colored citizens are not allowed to vote they will not by their numbers contribute to representative power, and one voter in South Carolina will not be able to neutralize two voters in Massachusetts or Illinois. Ex-rebels who had taken an oath to support the Constitution of the United States are excluded from office, national or state. The national debt is guaranteed, while the rebel debt and all claim for slaves are annulled. But all these essential safeguards are rudely rejected by the President.

The madness that would reject a proposition so essentially just, whose only error is its inadequacy, has broken forth naturally in brutal utterance, where he has charged persons by name with seeking his life, and has stimulated a mob against them. It is difficult to surpass the criminality of this act; but thus far the old Greek epigram has been verified :—

> "A viper bit a Cappadocian's hide,
> Envenomed by the bite the viper died."

Though the persons thus assailed have not yet suffered, the country has. The violence of the President has provoked violence. His words were dragon's teeth which have already sprung up armed men. Witness Memphis; witness New Orleans. Who can doubt that the President is the author of these tragedies ? Charles IX. of France was not more completely the author of the massacre of St. Bartholomew, than Andrew Johnson is the author of those recent massacres which now cry out for judgment. History records that the guilty king was pursued in the silence of night by the imploring voices of murdered men, mingled with curses and imprecations, while their ghosts stalked through his chamber, until he sweated blood from every pore ; and when he came to die, his soul, wrung with the tortures of remorse, stammered out to his attendant : "Ah ! nurse ! my good nurse ! what blood ! what murders ! Oh ! what bad councils I followed ! Lord God pardon me ! have mercy on me !" Like causes produce like effects. The blood at Memphis and New Orleans must cry out until it is heard, and a guilty President may suffer the same retribution which followed a guilty king.

The evil that he has done already is on such a scale that it is impossible to measure it, unless as you measure an arc of the globe. I doubt if in all history there is any ruler, who in the

3

same brief space of time has done so much. There have been kings and emperors, proconsuls and satraps, who have exercised a tyrannical power; but the facilities of communication now lend swiftness and extension to all evil influences, so that the President has been able to do in a year what in other days would have taken a life. Nor is the evil that he has done confined to any narrow spot. It is co-extensive with the Republic. Next to Jefferson Davis stands Andrew Johnson as its worst enemy. The whole has suffered; but it is the rebel region which has suffered most. He should have sent peace; instead, he sent a sword. Behold the consequences.

In the support of his cruel "policy" the President has not hesitated to use his enormous patronage. President Lincoln said, familiarly, that, as the people had continued him in office, he supposed they meant that others should be continued in office also; and he acted accordingly. He refused to make removals. But President Johnson thinks otherwise, and he announces in public speech that there must be "rotation in office;" and then warming in anger against all who do not sustain his "policy," he says that he will "kick them out." Men appointed by the martyred Lincoln are to be "kicked out" of office by his accidental successor, while pretending to sustain the policy of the martyr. The language of the President is most suggestive. He "kicks" the friends of his well-loved predecessor; and he also "kicks" the careful counsel of that well-loved predecessor, especially insisting that "we must build up from the sound material."

What Remains to be Done.

And now that I may give practical direction to these remarks, let me tell you plainly what must be done. In the first place, Congress must be sustained in its conflict with the *One Man Power*, and in the second place, ex-rebels must not be restored to power. Bearing these two things in mind the way will be easy. Of course, the constitutional amendment must be adopted. As far as it goes, it is well; but it does not go far enough. More must be done. Impartial suffrage must be established. A homestead must be secured to every freedman, if in no other way, through the pardoning power. If to these is added Education, there will be a new order of things, with liberty of the press, liberty of speech and liberty of travel, so that Wendell Phillips may speak freely in Charleston or Mobile. There is an old English play, which goes under the name of the four "P's." Our present desires may be symbolized by four "E's," standing for *Emancipation, Enfranchisement, Equality and Education.* Let these be secured and all else will follow.

I can never cease to regret that Congress has hesitated by proper legislation to assume a temporary jurisdiction over the whole rebel region. To my mind the power was ample and unquestionable, whether in the exercise of belligerent rights or in the exercise of rights derived directly from the Constitution itself. In this way everything needful might have been accomplished. In the exercise of this just jurisdiction the rebel communities might have been fashioned anew, and shaped to loyalty and virtue. The President lost a great opportunity at the beginning. Congress has lost another. But it is not too late. If indisposed to assume this jurisdiction by an enabling Act constituting provisional governments, there are many things which Congress may do, acting indirectly or directly. Acting indirectly, it may insist that Emancipation, Enfranchisement, Equality and Education shall be established as a condition precedent to the recognition of any State whose institutions have been overthrown by rebellion. Acting directly, it may, by constitutional amendment or by simple legislation, fix all these forever.

Impartial Suffrage must be Secured by the Nation and not left to the States.

You are aware, that from the beginning I have insisted upon Impartial Suffrage as the only certain guarantee of security and reconciliation. I renew this persistance and mean to hold on to the end. Every argument, every principle, every sentiment is in its favor. But there is one reason, which at this moment I place above all others ; it is the *necessity of the case.* You will require the votes of colored persons in the rebel States in order to sustain the Union itself. ' Without their votes you cannot build securely for the future. Their ballots will be needed in time to come much more than their muskets have been needed in time past. For the sake of the white Unionists in the rebel States and for their protection ; for the sake of the Republic itself, whose peace is imperilled, I appeal for justice to the colored race. Give the ballot to the colored citizen and he will be not only assured in his own rights, but he will be the timely defender of yours. It is by a singular Providence that your security is linked inseparably with the recognition of his rights. Deny him if you will. It is at your peril.

But it is said, leave this question to the States ; and State rights are pleaded against the power of Congress. This has been the cry,—at the beginning to prevent efforts against the Rebellion, and now, at the end, to prevent efforts against the revival of the Rebellion. Whichsoever way we turn we encounter this cry. But if you yield now, you will commit the very error of Buchanan, when at the beginning he declared that we could not " coerce " a State. Nobody doubts now that a State in rebellion may be " coerced ; " and to my mind it is equally clear that a State just emerging from rebellion may be " coerced " to that condition which is required by the public peace.

But there are powers of Congress, not derived from the rebellion, which are adequate to this exigency, and now is the time to exercise them and thus complete the work that has been begun. It was the Nation that decreed Emancipation, and the Nation must see to it, by every obligation of honor and justice, that Emancipation is secured. It is not enough that Slavery is abolished in name. The Baltimore platform, on which President Johnson was elected, requires " the utter and complete *extirpation* of Slavery from the soil of the Republic ; " but this can be accomplished only by the eradication of every inequality and caste, so that all shall be equal before the law.

Be taught by Russia. The Emperor there did not content himself with a naked Proclamation of Emancipation. He followed this glorious act with minute provisions securing to the freedmen rights of all kinds, as to hold property, to sue and testify in court, *to vote* and *to enjoy the advantages of education.* All this was secured by the same power which decreed emancipation.

Be taught also by England, speaking by her most illustrious statesmen, who solemnly warn us against trusting to any local authorities for justice to the colored race. I begin with Burke, who saw all questions with the intuitions of a statesman and expressed himself with the eloquence of the orator. Here are his words uttered in 1792 :—

" I have seen what the colonial legislatures have done in reference to the improvement of the condition of the negro. It is arrant trifling. They have done little, and that little is good for nothing, *because it does not carry with it the executory principle.*"

Should we leave this question to the States we should find that all that they did would be " arrant trifling," and that it would want " the executory principle."

This testimony of Edmund Burke was followed shortly afterwards by that of Canning, who in 1799, exclaimed,—

" There is something in the relation between the despot and his slave, which must vitiate and render nugatory and null whatever laws the former might make for the benefit of the latter ; which however speciously these laws might be framed, however well adapted they might appear to the evils which they were intended to alleviate, must infallably be marred and defeated in the execution."

Then again he says,—

" Trust not the masters of slaves in what concerns legislation for slavery ! However specious their laws may appear, depend upon it, they must be ineffectual in their application. It is in the nature of things that they should be so. Their laws can never reach, will never cure the evil. There is something in the nature of absolute authority, which makes despotism in all cases, and under all circumstances, an incompetent and untrue

executor even of its own provisions in favor of the objects of its power."
—*Canning's Speeches,* vol. 1, pp. 193, 194.

The same testimony was given at a later day by Brougham,
who, in one of his most remarkable speeches, while protesting
against· leaving to the colonies legislation for the freedmen,
expressed himself as follows :—

"I entirely concur in the observations of Mr. Burke, repeated and
more happily expressed by Mr. Canning, that the masters of slaves are not
to be trusted with making laws upon slavery ; that nothing they do is ever
found effectual ; and that if by some miracle they ever chance to enact a
wholesome regulation, it is always found to want what Mr. Burke calls *the
executory principle ;* it fails to execute itself."—*Brougham's Speeches,*
vol. 2, p. 219.

Such is the concurring testimony of these three statesmen-
orators, whose eloquent voices unite to warn us against trusting
the freedmen to their old masters.

Reason is in harmony with this authoritative testimony. Surely
it is not natural to suppose that people, who have claimed property
in their fellow-man—who have indulged that "wild and guilty
phantasy that man can hold property in man"—will become at
once the kind and just legislators of freedmen. It is contrary to
nature to expect it. Even if they have made up their minds to
Emancipation, they are, from inveterate habit and prejudice,
incapable of doing justice to the colored race. There is the
President himself, who once charmed the country and the age by
announcing himself as the "Moses" of their redemption ; and
yet he is now exerting all his mighty ·power against the establishment of those safeguards without which there can be no true
redemption. In the discussions of the day the old pro-slavery
spirit that was in him, with its hostility to principles and to men,
comes out anew ;—as on the application of heat, the old tunes
frozen up in the bugle of Baron Munchausen were set a-going
and broke forth freshly as when the bugle sounded before.
People do not change suddenly or completely. The old devils are
not all cast out at once. Even the best of converts sometimes
backslide. It is recorded by so grave a writer as Southey, in his
history of Brazil, that a venerable woman accustomed to consider
human flesh as an exquisite dainty, was converted to Christianity
while in extreme old age. The faithful missionaries strove at
once to minister to her wants and asked her if there was any
kind of food which she needed. To all which the venerable convert replied: "My stomach goes against everything ; there is but
one thing which I fancy I could touch ; if I had the little hand of
a little tender boy, I think I could pick the bones ; but woe is
me ! there is nobody to go out and shoot one for me !" In simi-
lar spirit our Presidential convert now yearns for a taste of those
odious pretensions which were a part of slavery.

Now when a person thus situated, with great responsibilities to his country and to history, bound by public professions and by political associations—who has declared himself against slavery and has every motive for perseverance to the end—when such a person openly seeks to preserve some of its odious pretensions, are we not admonished again how unsafe it would be to trust those old masters, who are under no responsibility and have given no pledges, with the power of legislating for freedmen? I protest against it.

I claim this power for the nation. If it be said that the power has never been exercised, then, I say, that the time has come when it should be exercised. I claim it on at least three several grounds.

(1.) There is the *Constitutional Amendment*, already adopted by the people, which invests Congress with plenary powers to secure the abolition of slavery,—aye, its *extirpation*, according to the promise of the Baltimore platform;—including the right to sue and testify in court, and the right also to vote. The distinction that has been attempted between what are called *civil* rights and *political* rights is a modern invention. These two words, "civil" and "political," in their origin have the same meaning. One is derived from the Latin and the other from the Greek. Each signifies that which pertains. to a *city* or *citizen*. Besides, if the elective franchise seem "appropriate" to assure the "extirpation" of slavery, Congress has the same power to secure this right which it has to secure the right to sue and testify in courts, which it has already done. Every argument, every reason, every consideration by which you assert the power for the protection of colored persons in what are called their *civil* rights, is equally strong for their protection in what are called their *political* rights. In each case you legislate to the same end, that the freedman may be maintained in that liberty which has so tardily been accorded to him, and the legislation is just as "appropriate" in one case as in the other.

(2.) There is also that distinct clause of the Constitution, requiring the United States "to guarantee to every State in the Union a *republican form of government.*" Here is a source of power as yet unused. The time has come for its use. Let it be declared, that a State which disfranchises any portion of its citizens by a discrimination in its nature insurmountable, as in the case of color, cannot be considered a republican government. The principle is obvious, and its practical adoption would ennoble the country and give to mankind a new definition of republican government.

(3.) But there is another reason which is with me peremptory. There is no discrimination of color in the allegiance which you require. Colored citizens, like white citizens, owe allegiance to the United States ; therefore, they may claim protection as an equivalent. In other words, allegiance and protection must be reciprocal. As you claim allegiance of colored persons, you must accord protection. One is the consideration of the other. And this protection must be in all the rights of citizens, civil and political. Thus again do I bring home to the National Government this solemn duty. If this has not been performed in times past, it has been on account of the tyrannical influence of slavery, which perverted our government. But, thank God! that influence has been overthrown. Vain are the victories of the war, if this influence continues to tyrannize over the National Government. Formerly the Constitution was interpreted always for Slavery. I insist that, from this time forward, it shall be interpreted always for Freedom. This is the great victory of the war, or rather it is the crowning result of all the victories.

One of the most important battles in the world's history was that of Tours, in France, where the Mohamedans, who had come up from Spain, for three days contended with the Christians under Charles Martel. On this battle Gibbon remarks, that, had the result been different, " perhaps the interpretation of the Koran would now be taught in the schools of Oxford, and her pulpits might demonstrate the sanctity and truth of the revelation of Mahomet." Thus was Christianity saved, and thus has Liberty been saved by our victories. Had the rebels prevailed, Slavery would have had voices everywhere, and even in the Constitution itself. But it is Liberty now that must have voices everywhere, and the greatest voice of all in the national Constitution and the laws made in pursuance thereof.

In this cause I cannot be frightened by words. There is a cry against " centralization," " consolidation," " imperialism," all of which are bad enough when dedicated to any purpose of tyranny. As the House of Representatives is renewed every two years, it is inconceivable to suppose that such a body, fresh from the people and about to return to the people, can become a tyranny, especially when it seeks safeguards for Human Rights. A government, inspired by Liberty, is as wide apart from tyranny as Heaven from Hell.. There can be no danger in Liberty assured by central authority ; nor can there be any danger in any powers to uphold Liberty. Such a centralization, such a consolidation,—aye, Sir, such an imperialism would be to the whole country a well-spring of security, prosperity and renown. To find danger in it is to find danger in the Declaration of Independence and the Constitution itself, which speak with central power ; it is to find danger in those central laws which govern the moral and material world, binding men together in society and keeping the planets wheeling in their spheres.

Often during the war the cause of our country seemed to appear in three different forms, each essential in itself and yet together constituting one unit. It was like the shamrock, or white clover, with its triple leaf, originally used to illustrate the Trinity. It, was Three in One. These three different forms were first, the national forces; secondly, the national finances; and thirdly, the ideas which entered into the controversy. The national forces and the national finances have prevailed. The ideas are still in question, and even now you debate with regard to the *rights of citizenship.* Nobody doubts that the army and navy fall plainly within the jurisdiction of the National Government, and that the finances fall plainly within the jurisdiction of the National Government; but the rights of citizenship are as thoroughly national as the army and navy or the finances. Obviously, you cannot without peril cease to regulate the army and navy; nor without peril cease to regulate the finances; but there is equal peril in abandoning the rights of citizens, who, wherever they may be, or in whatever .State, are entitled to protection from the Nation,—"the very least as feeling her care and the greatest as not exempted from her power." An American citizen in a foreign land enjoys the protecting hand of the National Government. He should not enjoy that protecting hand less at home than abroad.

Our Present Duty.

Fellow-citizens,—As I am about to close, allow me to gather the whole case into a brief compass. The President, wielding the *One Man Power,* has assumed a prerogative over Congress utterly unjustifiable, and has undertaken to dictate a fatal " policy " of reconstruction, which gives sway to rebels, puts off the blessed day of security and reconciliation, and leaves the best interests of the Republic in jeopardy. Treacherous to party—treacherous to the great cause—and treacherous to himself, he has set up his individual will against the people of the United States in Congress assembled. Forgetful of truth and decency, he has assailed members as " assassins," and has denounced Congress itself as a revolutionary body, "called or assuming to be Congress," and "hanging on the verge of government;" as if this most enlightened and patriot Congress did not contain the embodied will of the American people. To you, each and all, I appeal to arrest this madness. Your votes will be the first step. The President must be taught that usurpation and apostacy cannot prevail. He who promised to be Moses, and has become Pharaoh, must be overthrown, and the Egyptians that follow him must share the same fate, so that it shall be said now as aforetime, " And the Lord overthrew the Egyptians in the midst of the sea."

www.ingramcontent.com/pod-product-compliance
Lightning Source LLC
Chambersburg PA
CBHW021610270326
41931CB00009B/1416